DARK SHADES OF THE AMERICAN DREAM

To Timi,

Greatness is your
future

DARKER SHADES OF THE AMERICAN DREAM

Oba George, MD

BOOKLOGIX®

Alpharetta, GA

ISBN: 978-1-63183-260-4

Library of Congress Control Number: 2018902205

10 9 8 7 6 5 4 3 2   0 2 2 6 1 8

Printed in the United States of America

♾This paper meets the requirements of ANSI/NISO Z39.48-1992 (Permanence of Paper)

To my wife, Lize, and my wonderful parents, Tony and Beatrice. And to you, Gianella.

I can comprehend complex sciences that are undetectable with the naked eye and convey these intricacies with ease, but the capacity to readily appreciate another's perspective still eludes me.

—Oba George

CONTENTS

Preface xi

Acknowledgments xiii

Poor Soil...1

Weed: "A Plant in the Wrong Place" 7

Lonely Evolution 11

Biological Adaptations 15

Locusts 17

Essential Elements: Carbon, Oxygen, and Hydrogen 21

The Black Baccara Rose Is Perennially the Most Beautiful 25

Purposed toward the Sun 29

Ultraviolet Ray 35

Sweat and Tears to Stop Bleeding 39

Prey/Pray 47

Darkened Dreams 53

Subsisting without Sun 59

PREFACE

As a poor African American male, it was often difficult to obtain respect and challenging to discover avenues to ascend from poverty. Upon entering the middle class, my expectations for respect were tempered. After receiving my medical degree, obtaining collective acceptance and respect remain only dim dreams.

Now I desire only to share authentic anecdotes of my experiences in an attempt to engender a different perspective on the minority pursuit of American ideals. I harbor no hatred toward any persons or institutions and seek to generate constructive discussion rather than become a catalyst for further division.

ACKNOWLEDGMENTS

I would like to thank all my family, friends, and colleagues who have assisted me in this endeavor. Specifically, I thank my parents, Beatrice and Tony, for always believing in me; and my siblings, Helen, Agnes, and Isaac, for expecting the best from me. I also thank my wife, Lize, for always being my first, my most candid, and my harshest critic.

I thank my friends and colleagues Chantel, Richard, Quentin, Bryan, and Chris for spending their time reviewing the piece.

Lastly, I want to thank the BookLogix family for all their assistance with bringing this undertaking to fruition.

XIII

POOR SOIL

"Get out the street, nigger!"

Mike and I had ridden our bikes to the "Ghetto Kroger" a mile away. We would take these afternoon journeys, in the hot Georgia sun, to get ice cream and sports drinks if we could gather enough quarters and dimes. During the ride home, we had to cross a major intersection. The light turned red for adjacent oncoming traffic. The crossing light turned green. And while crossing the intersection, as fast as our adolescence allowed, I heard it.

An angry, raspy voice with a Southern disposition echoed over the sound of a loud pickup-truck engine.

"Get out the street, nigger!" he screamed again.

I looked over my right shoulder and found an elderly, white man with sun-cracked skin and yellow teeth glaring at me. He shook his decaying fists in the air and yelled it again. His white pickup truck was covered in mud and its skin was peeling.

Mike was white, so this man was obviously talking to me. It was my first time hearing that word used derogatorily toward me.

The early part of my child-

hood was spent in Norcross, Georgia, an impoverished area filled with blacks, Hispanics, and a few white people. Interestingly, even though all of us were poor, we still segregated ourselves. The Hispanics stayed toward the center of the community, the few whites stayed near the outskirts, and blacks filled the areas in between.

My siblings and I grew accustomed to taking brief, cold showers because, at times, the gas money was reallocated to pay rent. Creative variations of chicken-flavored ramen were a huge part of our after-school diet. I would "forget" to tell my parents about field trips to spare myself the disappointment. Allowances and family vacations were luxuries I only heard about.

My friends were blatant vendors of marijuana and its associates not only throughout the neighborhood but also at Tecker High. It seemed like every other teenage girl I knew was pregnant. Students were kicked out of classes routinely. Recurrent offenders relished the attention from their outbursts and went to the principal's office with zeal. Fistfights or straight-up "jumpings" were a social event. Students would show up late for the following period because we all had to watch the altercations to the end. How else would you be able to recount "who whooped who" when conversing with the other members of the student body?

My only solace was basketball. While my friends practiced the arts of the street hustle, I orchestrated grand plays on the court. I spent hours pounding pavement and refining my fundamentals. Fresh off a summer growth spurt, at six feet tall, I was unquestionably going to be the next Kobe Bryant. I diligently studied video footage of his moves and replicated them flawlessly in games. I played everybody in the neighborhood until I could decimate them all. I had to be the best.

Basketball was more than a recreational activity. To me, it was the answer. I was going to conquer the courts during basketball tryouts. I would make the varsity team as a freshman and average twenty points a game. All the colleges in the southeast would be obligated to take note and offer me full-ride scholarships. This would allow me to go anywhere I pleased, and I wouldn't have to burden my parents with college tuition fees. If I played my cards right, this round ball would transport me to a better place.

My parents did not share my athletic aspirations. My father was a gruff, no-nonsense, ex-military man who had no time for games. He held two jobs for eleven years. He worked as a technician during the day and was an overnight manager at a chemical plant. If he took time away from sleep to have a "talk" with you, there was minimal talking involved. "Go and get the belt." "Go and get a switch." These swift judgments and penalties were decreed with frequency in the George household.

My mother was a God-fearing, petite woman. She made up for her short stature with an omniscient personality and a sharp, authoritative voice. She was fair and understanding but would send you to the judge if your atrocities were too severe.

Unbeknownst to my three siblings and I, my parents toiled and scraped for years so we could move to a "good neighborhood." Long ago, they realized this neighborhood did not lend itself to strong family values or encourage kids in the way of educational advancement. "Education is most important," my mother would say. "You can dribble that ball all day, scrape your knees, and sweat, but they can't take what's in your head!"

The next year, we moved to Lawrenceville, Georgia.

WEED: "A PLANT IN THE WRONG PLACE"

Huge gated communities equipped with royal-blue pools and manicured lawns were all filled with families who looked like they belonged on a post card. Everyone recycled. My parents' years of hard labor had finally positioned us for a piece of the American Dream.

At school, students advertised for designer clothes daily, which reminded others they were among the social elite. Fresh luxury and sports vehicles lined the student parking lot. The "Good Mall," with the brand-name stores, was where those who mat-tered rendezvoused after school. It was a predominantly white area where seeing other minorities was a rarity. I and the other handful of black kids in my class became fast friends.

A few months after the move, my father and I took a presumed quick trip to Kroger to pick up some groceries. On our return, a black patrol car with aging light fixtures began to follow us. Initially, we did not think much of the event. But after about five minutes, we still had our unrequested police escort.

"I wasn't speeding? We didn't run a light?" my dad questioned aloud.

He gripped the weathered black steering wheel with both of his cracked hands. Perspiration appeared over his tense, wrinkled forehead. Anxiety entered my stomach and my heartbeat became audible. We both remained stiff and breathing became more difficult.

My father and I stared straight ahead, out the cracked windshield, as though this would change our pursuer's mind. Our silence was broken by the sound of the patrol car's sirens and the sight of red and blue lights in our rear view.

We pulled over to the right side of the deserted highway, and the patrol car followed into the gravel. My father remained still. My heart tried to penetrate my chest. A stoic, hefty officer with dark sunglasses and dark hair slowly approached us, his steps progressively becoming louder. A stern face leaned in my father's window with his flashlight and exposed nothing but fear.

He demanded, "License and registration," barely moving his lips.

My dad opened the glove

box with a slight tremor and removed the documents. While placing them in the cop's outstretched hands, he inadvertently dropped the insurance card on the driver's seat.

"S-sorry," my father stuttered said awkwardly and looked up at the officer. The officer nodded to imply it was okay to retrieve the card. Without any further words, he took the documents back to his patrol car. And we waited in silence.

Was our taillight broken? Our insurance outdated? We began to question what we had done to deserve this unexpected encounter on a Sunday afternoon.

The officer returned a few minutes later and said, "We are looking for two men who just robbed a local Kmart."

My father and I looked at him, perplexed. Then we both expressed a silent rage that was not lost on our provocateur.

"Aa-ite now, you guys be careful." He presented us with our papers and told us we could leave.

My father sighed despairingly and looked down at the violated documents in his lap. Then he turned to me and said, "This America is not right. That's how they ruin black men. You have a bright future. You don't want to get caught up in the system. You have to stay out of trouble because you have a target on your back."

LONELY EVOLUTION

Out of all the sciences, biology came most natural to me. It made sense. Life's various adaptations to survive were logical. First, organisms evolved to become the finest version of themselves. Then, they passed these superior characteristics and enhanced resources to their offspring through genetics. This profound ingenuity ensures that their children will have the quality attributes needed to succeed and flourish.

Back in Norcross, my parents saw a dying environment surrounded by negative portrayals of life. They knew this dry soil would not support healthy children. Through hard work they were able to place us in a fertile, healthy school system with an abundance of resources, and we flourished academically.

My father would always present our options as college versus infinite years of poverty, regret, and disgrace. "You have a great opportunity. Don't waste it," he would grimly remind us.

I was still six feet tall, and my basketball peers were now looking down on me. I decided to drop my basketball and pick up a book.

"You talk proper." He

shook his dreadlocks as though that was not what he had meant to say. "I mean you talk white, you know what I mean?" He searched my eyes, to see if offense had been taken.

He kept repositioning the gold-plated grill covering his lower row of teeth. The whites of his eyes were reddened and barely visible. A thick aroma of herbal influence encircled us. He was wearing what at one time had likely been a white shirt but was now closer to beige. We were in the "other" part of town, visiting our cousins for the summer. There were four kids and they lived in a two-bedroom apartment.

I shrugged.

"You tryna go to college, huh?" He asked as though he had discovered the answer midsentence.

"Yeah," I replied.

His sister and her friend, who were across the street, joined us on the porch to invade our "deep" conservation.

"My friend said you probably gon marry a white girl," his sister giggled. "She said she thinks you're cute."

I tried to make my smile casual while glancing at her friend. She had deep purple hair and long, thin braids. Her full, dark complexion sparkled in the south Georgia sun. Her eyes were large and milk-chocolate brown. They kept my attention for longer than I anticipated. She smiled at me, which produced another smile on my face.

"Aye, college boi! Keep reading dem books, my nigga!" my male cousin interjected. He had interrupted my trance. "I'm out here getting this money in these streets. But you might get paid from dem books too."

BIOLOGICAL ADAPTATIONS

"We're all going to meet up at my parents' lake house later. You should come!"

Becky, one of my newly obtained white friends, was inviting me to a "chillhang" after school to help me gain social capital. No doubt this adventure would include alcohol and marijuana, among other temptations.

I was mesmerized by her beach-blue eyes. "I don't know about all that."

She smiled at me through her clear braces. "Come on, it'll be fun!" She said it while literally twisting my arm.

I looked at her crew-cut sweater and then down at the ground. My faded grey sneakers were cracking at the soles. They reminded me this was a bad idea. My eyes found hers again and I mustered a lie.

"Sure."

This particular invitation and others like it made me uncomfortable. Not because I thought she was too popular to associate with the new black guy at a predominantly white school. Actually, this would likely enhance her social net worth. It was not because I believed she thought less of me than I expected. In fact, I was relatively confident that over the last three days

she had been flirting with me. And it was also not because it was improbable that her parents had entrusted an unsupervised lake house to their daughter and several other fickle, misguided adolescents.

It was because it was well known at McCutter High School that at these racially curious events, when youthful exuberance became criminal (which was frequently), the cops were called. And when police arrived, "I" and others like "me" seemed to attract most of law enforcement's interest and consequently most of its repercussions.

Many "Jamals," "Tyrones," and others had been arrested, suspended, and even expelled after getting caught drinking underage or in possession of illegal substances while attending one of these mixed-raced shindigs. However, most of their fellow Caucasian imbibers and illicit consumers remained functional members of our student body and, at worst, received warnings.

LOCUSTS

After school, I began working at McDonald's to help support my family. For apathetic or angry customers, I would construct their favorite cheeseburgers, "drop the fries," and count out their change with an artificial smile. My uniform was a dark-green shirt with two bright-yellow vertical lines and some tattered khakis. Both kept a dense perfume of burger-patty grease, freshly salted fries, and yesterday's sweat. Cleaning foul-smelling, soiled toilets and taking out soaked-through trash bags were some of my "favorite" tasks.

I would serve America's golden addiction until 10:30 or 11:00 p.m. most weekdays. Gladly, I would pick up "doubles" on the weekend and work from 6:00 a.m. to 6:30 p.m. My goal was to work enough hours to cross into that glorious overtime pay.

I began paying the electric bill, the gas bill, or "putting something on the rent" to alleviate some of my parents' financial strain. Four mouths to feed and a newly acquired lower, middle-class mortgage were enough to stress our finances and our family dynamic. When you came of age in the George household, it was an unstated rule that you

were going to get a job and contribute.

After about a year, I was able to save up for a car. A used, dark-green 1990 Honda Accord was one of the few vehicles compatible with my malnourished bank account. Its green hood was peeling and exposed areas of a metallic grey undercoating. A tiny rock was lodged in the top left corner of the windshield and a long, thin crack emanated southward. Its passenger side door did not open from the outside. It required the driver to lean over and unlock it from inside. The AC blew lukewarm to hot air. Most of the buttons on the front panel were just there for show. The center console was a faded brown and sat off-center. It did not close properly.

It was my first car and it got me to and from work . . . most of the time.

"Let me hold fifty dollars, man," he asked and demanded at the same time.

Stephen, my dad's work friend, had come to visit— again. I never really understood why. A large man, but he was vertically deficient. His essence was all in his stomach. He was balding and possessed a huge gap in the center of his crooked teeth. He always had a toothpick in his mouth and he always had a story. He filled the air with fabrications like he was getting paid for it. Presumably, he was.

"I use to have hundreds of thousands dollars before my wife left me" or "I use to be in business for myself" were a few of his most frequent story lines. However, for the last seven years I knew him, he worked with my dad at a data-gathering company. And he was always asking us for money.

"I don't got it right now," I lied. Well, I was lying to a fraud, so my conscience did not bother me. I had about one hundred and twenty dollars in my account. I was hoping to eventually have my car's AC fixed or just be able to cover its next broken part.

"Why are you always so stingy? You know I'm good for it," Steve said. This was also a falsehood. He had fooled me on one occasion several months prior and still owed me a hundred dollars.

"What about the hundred dollars you owe me?" I retorted.

He grinned, like he knew this statement was coming. "We'll make it one hundred and fifty dollars. I'll add interest. I'll give you a cool one-fifty, next time I see you. You know what interest is, don't you?"

My dad came down the stairs wearing a navy-blue polo, name tag, and khakis. It was time for work. He was unaware of the buffoonery taking place in his living room prior to his presence.

"Steve, you ready to go?" my father asked.

Stephen looked at me coyly like he had just been having a "normal" conversation with a close friend's son. I repaid his look with a familiar disappointment that I displayed openly on my face.

"Yeah," Stephen said. And they left for work.

ESSENTIAL ELEMENTS: CARBON, OXYGEN, AND HYDROGEN

By senior year of high school, I was obsessed with getting into college. College had transplanted all my other aspirations. It was the only guarantee for my ascension to the good life. I accumulated a 3.8 grade point average, was selected to attend several advanced-placement courses, and my SAT scores were above average. To me, these were minor investments for the wealth and respect my college degree would return.

I applied to a historically black college, Howard University. I also applied to Georgia State University and the University of Georgia. I questioned whether going to a predominantly black college would enhance or stifle my career trajectory.

Did my potential future employers think less of historically black colleges? I pontificated. Or would going to a large, diverse college like the University of Georgia open more occupational doors? If I did, well, should it even matter?

I accepted my invitation to

Georgia State University, because the tuition was cheaper.

"D = M/V," he scribbled on the chalkboard.

The class continued to chatter, and most students were oblivious to the fact that the professor had arrived. The professor was an aged, self-assured black man with a well-groomed, salt-and-pepper afro. Large brown glasses, which he'd brought with him from the seventies, shielded his eyes. He turned and faced the class with a look of heavy annoyance. The class continued to converse. He folded his arms and said nothing for about a minute while searching for a target.

"All right, so you there. What is this equation?" The professor's words broke up multiple conversations. The students quieted. His question and eyes were directed at me.

I asked, "Me?" while stupidly pointing to myself. A few students laughed.

"Yes, you! What does the equation represent?" he replied.

"Uh . . . density equals mass over volume," I said.

A subtle grin crept onto his face. I supposed he was pleased someone had read the first chapter. He turned around and continued to write on the board. The lecture began.

Over the next several weeks, I would attend all Dr. Karr's chemistry lectures, complete all extra-credit assignments, and organize frequent meetings with him. In our meetings, we would discuss chemical bonds and energy transference, but slowly we introduced life chemistry as well. He had a direct demeanor, but he would always make sure I understood why that day's lesson was important.

"Brother, vision precedes any major success," he would say, looking over his retro specs. "What are you going to do with your life?" he asked frequently. "You're a smart black man. You have to go get what you want in this life. Nobody is going to give it to you." Each message was the most important until the next one.

My second year of college and long after I had left Chemistry 1101, he gave me a job as a teacher's assistant. I would also assist new interns in his chemistry lab. The small cash flow sponsored milk, cereal, and bath soap in my college dorm room. It also helped finance my college "extracurriculars" over the weekends. He impressed upon me the importance of family after he endured a devastating divorce a few years earlier. "Cherish and nurture the relationships that matter," he would muse. It was the only time he looked vulnerable.

Dr. Karr would call and check on me every few weeks throughout college. He always wanted to ensure that I never lost my immense fervor to succeed.

THE BLACK BACCARA ROSE IS PERENNIALLY THE MOST BEAUTIFUL

"What's her name again?" Frank asked while staring directly at her.

"Isabel," I answered.

"Yeah, that's right!" he responded. Frank had already met Isabel earlier in the night. He was drunk and had already forgotten her name. I was slightly less inebriated.

"She's hot, and she's a nurse!" he stated emphatically. He apparently remembered bits and pieces of his prior conversation with her.

I was celebrating my twenty-first birthday and had invited my family, current college friends, and remaining high school friends. Frank was one of my college friends. We shared several biology and chemistry courses together. Isabel was one of my few residual high school friends.

Isabel and I had become friends in high school initially because she was friends with my sister. The two used to deliberate fashion trends and boyfriend predicaments in my sister's room after school.

"He's just going to do it again! I would leave him," my sister would advise. I always wondered why someone as

gorgeous as Isabel would let various "cool guys" waste her time.

Isabel was truly stunning. Her seductive brown eyes were hypnotic. She had a big, glowing smile that was irresistible and complemented her tall, slender figure. She possessed a genuine laugh that produced itself effortlessly. Her gentle cocoa complexion always looked perfect in any light. And her magnetic personality made everyone instantly adore her.

She had given me her number when I had gone off to college. And with this act, she had sparked a deep friendship that would persist for years. Frequently, we stayed up to two in the morning discussing all our naïve aspirations and goals. For instance, she would prophesy she was "going to be married by twenty-five," whereas I just wanted to be happily married at some point. She wanted to be a young, affluent business executive "living in a high-rise in New York City." All I wanted was to provide for my fictional future family, and I was open to living anywhere with warm weather.

A year after I left high

school, she began attending a neighboring college, Kennesaw State University. Quick lunches, long dinners, and catching the latest superhero films had been some of our most frequent endeavors. She introduced me to Thai food and I introduced her to Vietnamese pho.

She would go on to date other imposters from time to time. I always regarded her as being within the upper echelon of potential girlfriends. I had given up long ago on the fruitless pursuit of someone who was obviously out of my league.

"She's actually seeing somebody right now," I fabricated. I was unsure if she was, but I was going to find out.

I left Frank standing by himself without ending the conversation. I trotted toward Isabel with a confidence that only came by way of intoxication. Isabel was sitting at a table laughing with some of my female college friends. She was unaware of the tornado of inebriated ignorance that was en route.

I staggered to her table and tapped on her left shoulder. There was no turning back now. The whole table watched intently. They were interested in what the drunk birthday boy had to say.

Isabel was surprised to see me standing over her shoulder.

I looked into her brown eyes, and they caused me to stutter. "W-w-would you like to go on a real date? Like, not as friends, but a real date?"

Isabel's expression morphed from surprise to amazement. Then, she smiled bashfully. Most of the onlookers sat in uncomfortable silence. A few covered their mouths in shock and awe.

Isabel stood up slowly, kissed me on my right cheek, and whispered, "I thought you would never ask."

PURPOSED TOWARD THE SUN

"So, what are you going to do?" my mother questioned. Her back was turned to me and she was battling a large, silver pot in the kitchen sink. I had stopped by on an innocent Sunday evening in the pursuit of a free, homecooked meal.

"I don't know. I'll probably get a PhD in biology. I could be a professor and teach. I'm not really sure," I replied.

It then occurred to me she was asking not because she wanted my answer but rather because she had something to say. I quickly opened the fridge and started looking for something small and portable.

"Whatever you do, you have to be the best!" she followed. She finished rinsing the pot and placed it on the nearby drying rack. I began to pray within that these were her closing remarks.

"Yes, Mommmm," I replied. I rolled my eyes and sighed, making sure to remain out of her field of vision. At this point, I closed the fridge. I was thinking about just making a run for it.

"You could be a doctor, or even the president! You have a gift and a calling. Find it, and make a difference." She was now staring intently at me and standing in the kitchen door-

way. She wanted to emphasize her point and cut off my potential escape route. She was likely aware of my quiet plotting.

"Okay. I understand. I will." I kissed her on her left cheek.

She cut her eyes at me with partial contentment and left the kitchen. She had delivered her sermon and was now off to deliver another message to a different member of her congregation.

I spent the next summer attempting to observe doctors in Lawrenceville, Georgia.

My first attempt was a lo-cal pediatrician. I drove to her clinic on a dry, summer afternoon. I decided to park my actively decomposing Honda in the back of the parking lot next to two large, mustard-yellow dumpsters. Hopefully, this would prevent people from associating me with the sound of faulty, high-squealing brakes. I was wearing my dad's oversized grey slacks and a pressed white button-up. The armpits were saturated, as I had no air conditioning to defend me from the pitiless Georgia sun. I walked in with a good amount of uncertainty. I was not really sure how to go about this. I was asking a random medical doctor to allow me to spend time in her clinic. I swallowed some of my trepidation and proceeded.

I spoke briefly with the young, soft-spoken receptionist at the front desk.

"Have a seat and the doctor will be with you shortly," she said.

I found an empty seat in the lobby. The receptionist then disappeared into the back.

A few moments later, a petite white lady with short brunette hair and a Dora the Explorer stethoscope around her neck entered the lobby. Her confident smile helped me conclude that she was the pediatrician.

"Hey, I'm George. Um, I would like to spend some time in your clinic to learn more about medicine. I'm thinking about becoming a doctor," I stated.

She shook my outstretched hand. "I don't think that should be a problem. I'll just have to review the office's insurance coverage to make sure they will allow me to have an observer. A staff member or I will call you in a few days."

"Thanks so much," I replied. I shook her hand again and graciously left my phone number before leaving the clinic.

For the first time, I began to truly believe that this broke black kid from Norcross, Georgia, could make a name for himself. I could be "Dr. George." That would be something. I would wear crisp button-ups and sharp slacks every day. Everyone would respect me. My first purchase would obviously be a brand-new, all-black Audi. I would welcome the fresh leather seats and infinite frosty air conditioning. I went home and informed my parents that this dream was almost tangible.

A week went by, and I did not hear back from her office. I assumed the pediatrician was too busy or had just forgotten. After all, she was a doctor. The next day, I drove back to her facility to courteously ask about the status of my request. When I arrived at the front desk, a cruel and grey medical assistant informed me that "someone has filled the position" and promptly continued to surf the web. The young, sweet receptionist from my previous visit was nowhere to be found. When I asked to speak with the doctor,

I was told by the grim, ancient one that "she is busy and will not be seeing any nonscheduled appointments today" in an abrasive tone.

I returned three more times and was told variations of the same. My numerous phone calls were never returned.

My second attempt was with a nearby internal-medicine doctor's practice. I visited his office on a quiet Monday morning. I spoke initially with his adolescently exuberant receptionist and inquired about a potential observership.

"I don't know what that is, but if you wait over there, I'll ask him," she snapped.

Most of the seats were occupied by waiting patients, so I sat in the back of the lobby. After thirty minutes went by, an aged white man with a few strands of grey hair appeared. He was wearing a long, pristine white coat and walked as though the world around him were moving much too slowly.

I assumed he was the doctor. He spoke to his receptionist for a moment. She pointed at me, but her words were inaudible. Presumably, she was relaying my request.

He glanced in my direction too swiftly to obtain eye contact and then turned back to his receptionist. They conversed for a few more seconds as though the subject of their conversation was not watching them communicate. Suddenly, the doctor turned toward me and belted from across the lobby, "We don't do that here!" and promptly returned to his office.

The patrons in the lobby pretended to not stare. But I could still feel their eyes. Wearing a heavy cloak of humiliation, I stood up and left.

I asked every family-medicine doctor, cardiologist, and surgeon in town who would pick up the phone. I was repeatedly told no or received no response altogether. I searched online in medical-student blogs and websites to determine how others got exposure to the medical field. I realized most of these students had family members or friends who were doctors. But I had no one.

ULTRAVIOLET RAY

"So you're just going to give up?" she asked while peering at me through her brown bifocals. Her voice possessed a challenge that irritated my pride.

"I'm not giving up. No one will let me spend time in their clinic. I'm just accepting reality." I folded my arms and looked at the ground.

My aunt Grace and I were both sitting at the old coffee table and she was having her evening tea. She was a wise and lively old woman who did not hold her tongue. While she was visiting this weekend, my mother had told her, and just about everyone else, that I no longer aspired to be a doctor.

Aunt Grace wanted to "speak with me" because she had strong opinions about my dream abandonment.

"Well, nothing worth having is easily obtained," she replied. She took a long sip of her steaming tea and leaned back in her chair.

"Okay?" I stared blankly at her. She could read on my face that I didn't believe her timely words of wisdom were going to get me an observership with a local doctor.

She placed her mug on the coffee table and sighed. "What I'm trying to say is, it's going to be hard sometimes, but you have to persevere." She gently

placed her left hand on my shoulder. "I know a really nice black trauma surgeon. I'll give him a call. He'll probably let you spend some time with him."

I looked up at her with my arms still folded. I was not very confident in this outcome. "Thanks," I replied halfheartedly.

Astonishingly, the following week Dr. JaMichael invited me to spend time with him in the operating room and in his clinic.

For the rest of that summer and the next, I would see crying victims of motorcycle accidents with broken legs, errant gunshot wounds to abdomens with life-threatening hemorrhaging, and even drunken falls off roofs with shattered spines. Our patients and their family members would come into the emergency department with hopeless, broken dispositions. We would take severely damaged patients to the operating room, meticulously clean out their wounds, and literally sew them back together. Many perished. Sometimes, if we were lucky, we could stop the bleeding, bones would heal, and we would eventually see them restored. Watching distraught and fractured families reunite with their newly repaired loved ones was an irreplaceable experience. It was the most fulfilling thing I had ever done.

The last patient I saw that summer was a young black teenager, John. I spent a lot of time speaking with John. He was seventeen years old, a straight-A student, and was about six feet tall. More than anything he loved playing basketball. He was on a traveling team and played small forward for the Baradale Blaze. He liked Kobe Bryant but idolized Lebron James.

Unfortunately, earlier that Saturday, his little brother had been playing with his father's loaded shotgun and it mistakenly discharged. The blast had removed several inches of skin, muscle, and bone from John's right shoulder and neck. John had to undergo several major surgeries.

Before one of his most life-threatening procedures, he looked at me with tears flowing down his face and said, "I'm scared. Am I going to die?"

"We are going to do our best to get you healthy, and we are here for you," I responded. My voice cracked and I fought back my own tears. I touched his left shoulder. And then he slowly wiped his tears.

SWEAT AND TEARS TO STOP BLEEDING

"Dog, are you serious? Are you really tryna be a doctor?" Daunte asked with shock and bewilderment permeating his voice. We were walking down the hallway to our Wednesday afternoon biochemistry lecture.

"Yeah man. I can't think of anything better. I'm using science to actually help people." My reply caused Daunte to stop walking and look away like he had tasted something sour.

"Yeah, but you're going to be in school forever!" he replied. His look and tone emphasized this was an obvious quandary in not only his mind but to any normal person.

Daunte was one of my few black friends also taking advanced chemistry and biology courses. He was much smarter than me and would frequently beat my potential highest score on our organic-chemistry exams. He decided intern year that he wanted to be a pharmacist. He would always remind me that "in about four more years I'll be making 100K." This was likely why he was appalled by our current conversation.

"I get that," I responded. "But I don't want to be a phar-

macist a few years from now taking orders from the doctor, all the while thinking, *I could have been a doctor.*"

He shrugged and we resumed our pace to class. A sly grin emerged on the right side of his face. "Well, doctors do make stupid money," he remembered aloud.

He conceded the conversation point for now. He would tolerate my prolonged, foolish pursuits, if only because it garnered "stupid money."

I dedicated my last two years of college to getting into medical school.

I attended intricate lectures on physics, biochemist-ry, and calculus during the mornings and studied for the *dream-stealing* Medical College Admission Test (MCAT) at night. The MCAT is a laborious, eight-hour standardized exam that mercilessly pilfers the aspirations of potential doctors everywhere. To get into medical school one not only has to pass the devious exam, but also must outshine other competitive candidates for a highly coveted medical-school position.

On Thursdays, I would finish my organic-chemistry lectures at noon. Then, I'd grab two dollar-menu cheeseburgers from McDonald's on the corner and walk four blocks to meet with Olga.

Olga was a group MCAT tutor. She was an uncompromising, older Romanian woman with a deep Eastern European accent. Olga enjoyed locking group members out of her tutorial sessions for even one minute of tardiness. Many were victimized. Somehow, I only succumbed to this fate once. She provided thirty-page syllabi, ten pages of homework, and expected "pop quizzes" every time we met.

For the next two months, I woke up in drool-stained, test-taking strategy books. It was not uncommon for me to draw complex chemical pathways on napkins while forcing myself to eat dinner. I even began to have dreams about constructing molecules and their anatomic chemical structures. To obtain my dream job, a lifetime of respect, and to never have to worry about money again, I was willing to sacrifice sleep and my early twenties.

By my last semester of college, I wrestled away a 3.9 science grade point average and fortuitously secured a national average MCAT score. My ascension was all but assured. I was going to medical school. I began to envision "Dr.

George" stitched perfectly into my very own crisp, white coat. I confidently applied to all the medical schools in Georgia.

Two weeks later, I received email notification that two of the institutions had placed me on a waiting list. I received a rejection letter from a third. "Waitlisted" meant I was considered but not automatically invited to attend their medical schools. Other, "more competitive" candidates would have to refuse their invitations for me to get a spot. My dream was evaporating, and I wept internally.

Early the next morning, I frantically drove to the nearest medical school, Deblank Georgia Medical. I hoped maybe meeting someone in person, within the admissions office, would bring me favor. I had to exhaust every opportunity I could.

A small white woman with short, white hair and a large, warm smile greeted me at the front desk.

"What can I do for you, hun?" she asked with thick Southern charm.

Nancy Pritchers was the secretary to the dean of admissions. I would find out later that she had held that position for the last fifteen years, and while she was not an active member of the admissions committee, her opinions still carried weight.

"Morning, I'm Oba George. I'm one of the wait-listed candidates for this year's medical-school class. I just wanted to come in and ask if there was anything I could do to increase my chances of getting into the medical school. I'm willing to do whatever it takes." I looked her bravely in the eye.

"I understand. Well, right now we are still reviewing applications, but we will know in two weeks," she replied. Her tone convinced me she had had this conversation several times today with other candidates.

"Okay, well, I'll check back in a few days. Thanks." My disappointment was evident in my voice. I shook her hand and left.

I called the admissions office and by default spoke to Nancy Pritchers three times a week for the next two weeks. I called so often she began to recognize my voice on the telephone. I even made two more visits to Deblank Medical School "just to say hello" to Nancy. I would always address her as "ma'am" and be sure to thank her for her time at the end of our conversations. She was always polite and tolerated my chronic pestering gracefully.

Two weeks later, while watching *House* on my living-room couch, I received a phone call from an assistant professor at the school. I nearly fell off the couch while speaking to him. I was officially invited to attend Deblank Georgia Medical School!

My heart smiled radiantly that day. I was going to be a doctor! I was going to be able help heal people and be respected. My family would never have to worry about money again. I shared the news with all my family and friends. Pride and excitement filled the George household. It was the happiest day of my life.

Possessed by my excitement, I sporadically drove to the medical school to visit Nancy. I just wanted to thank her for tolerating all my "annoyances" through the last several weeks.

I found Nancy slowly packing her unorganized office into several labeled, cardboard boxes. Her desk was cleared. The walls were bare. She did not look up to see who had entered her office as I shut the door behind me. She quietly continued to sort documents.

"Hey," I started. "Is everything okay?"

She looked up. "I'm going to be leaving the medical school." She had a concerning distance in her eyes.

"Oh, I'm sorry to hear that," I replied. "I got in. I just wanted to say thanks for, you know, everything."

She looked at me calmly, and then a half-hearted grin developed on her face. "That's good. That's real good."

"Well, I hope everything works out well," I stated solemnly. I followed with an awkward hug. For some reason I felt she required one.

"It's cancer. I have cancer. I'm going to be with my family," she whispered in my left ear.

I released her from my embrace and looked at her. She had a painful calmness about her. My initial shock quickly became pity. No words could be found. I honestly didn't know what to say. I started to say I was sorry, but she interrupted.

"I told them they should let you in. I told 'em," she said. "You are going to make a fine doctor."

My eyelids became heavy and my eyes watered. I found myself trying not to cry, as she was the one who had received devastating news. I embraced her closer and pretended to be strong for her in that moment. But inside I was deeply shaken.

This frail, elderly white lady had fought on my behalf to get me into medical school. Why would she help me? I couldn't understand. And the realization that Nancy had just obtained this grave diagnosis engendered an immense, genuine sadness that overwhelmed me. A tear escaped my control and ran free down my right cheek.

PREY/PRAY

"It's Dad," he said softly. He paused for an uncomfortable amount of time. I sat up in bed and pressed my cell phone firmly to my right ear.

"I don't know what's wrong with him," he continued.

My brother Isaac's phone call had woken me up me at 11:40 p.m. on a school night. My imagination autopopulated only the worst possible scenarios. My heart fluttered and I promptly stood up next to my bed.

"What's wrong," I demanded. Would I never see my father alive again? What was I going to do? I had to go home. Disjointed questions and terrible answers flooded my mind. My hands began to sweat and I tried to grip the cell phone tighter.

"I don't know. He just yelled out while I was sleeping. When I came into his room, he was on the floor gripping his chest. I called an ambulance." His voice revealed his unease, and he spoke as though he were asking me if he had done the right thing.

"Okay. I'm on my way," I responded. I slammed my cell phone shut and forced my legs through my nearest pair of jeans. I grabbed my keys off the kitchen counter and ran without restraint to my Honda.

In my lonely vehicle, I dashed down the dark highways

that would take me to my father. My imagination followed me.

He's probably had a heart attack. People live through those, right? Is my dad dead? Tears ran down my face. Genuine fear occupied the totality of my being.

Loud, cutting police sirens snapped me out of my devastating thoughts. I glanced in my rearview and found an imminent white-and-black patrol car. Blue and red lights instilled a new, different fear within me.

I pulled over to the right side of the highway and parked. The patrol car pursued. I wiped the tears from my eyes and tried to pretend I was composed.

Why was this happening to me? Why now? What did I do to deserve this? I don't think I was speeding, but I was not sure with everything that was happening.

After several moments, a middle-aged white man with a dark, thick mustache tapped on my window with a black flashlight.

"License and registration," he said. He sighed as though he was frustrated before our encounter had even begun.

"Yes, sir," I answered. I slowly took my hands off the steering wheel and opened my glove box. I pulled out the necessary documents and cautiously provided them to him.

"Um, sir, my father is being

taken to the hospital," I stated. It halted his retreat to his vehicle. "I would just like to know what I did, because my father is sick."

After all, I did not know why he pulled me over. I also hoped that perhaps today this information would produce some mercy given the circumstances.

"I ran your tag and your insurance is not current. You can't drive here without insurance," he responded. He then continued his trek back to his vehicle with my documents in hand. Our conversation was apparently over.

I grabbed one of the insurance pamphlets in my glove compartment and dialed the 1-800 number. I wrestled with the automated options for about two minutes and eventually was allowed to speak with a representative.

"Yes, Mr. George, I'm showing that it was renewed after an auto payment today. Your policy is showing as active here in our system," the sales associate assured me.

"I was just pulled over, and the cop doesn't believe I have insurance. Could you do me a huge favor and tell him what you just told me?" I asked.

"Sure! I'd be glad to, Mr. George," she responded.

Relief settled in. He would have to let me go and listen to

reason now. I placed the insurance representative on hold and waited for the law-enforcement agent. He returned to my left window a few minutes later.

"Sir, I have the insurance agent on the phone, and she states that my insurance is current. She says she can talk directly with you." I held the phone in front of me with my left hand to make it easier for the officer to take it and speak with her.

He looked at me for a moment and then looked at the phone in my outstretched hand.

"Now, we are not allowed to do that. I have what I have in my system. I go by that," he explained. "You can't drive without insurance. You're going to have to leave the car here and have someone pick you up."

"If you would just speak to the agent——" I started. He just stared at me blankly and shook his head. He had no interest in my words. He produced a pink citation covered in scribbled black ink. He walked back to his car and waited behind my vehicle. I suspected he was waiting for me to call a ride.

A mixture of misery and rage boiled inside me. I punched the steering wheel repeatedly in anger. Why me? After a minute or so, the thought of my father dying brought me to action. I picked up my cell phone and called my girlfriend Isabel to come and liberate me. I passionately described the details of my current "detainment" to her.

After she arrived, we made our way to the hospital to visit my father. He had survived a triple-bypass heart surgery earlier in the night after suffering a massive heart attack. We found him sleeping peacefully in his hospital bed. The doctor and nurses assured us he was going to be okay.

I sat next to his hospital bed and watched over my wounded father for hours. The strong ex-military man lay vulnerable in a faded hospital gown with wires inserted throughout his still body. *I don't know what I would have done. I'm not ready,* I thought. Isabel embraced me and placed her head on my chest. I closed my eyes and sighed painfully.

DARKENED DREAMS

"The patient in 501 asked if he . . . he could have a different doctor," the nurse sheepishly finished her sentence.

A few other doctors and several nurses also occupied the hectic southwest nursing station. The persistent dinging of patient bed alarms and indistinct nurse chatter drowned out her voice. I assumed she was talking to someone else and continued to type my last patient note. I did not look up from my computer.

"Doctor, the patient in 501—" she continued as she walked directly in front of my desk.

I stopped charting and glanced over the top edge of my grey computer monitor.

A tall, baby-faced white nurse was playing with the smooth silver cross at the end of her thin necklace. She flipped it back and forth in her left hand. Her gaze was focused on the ground. She sighed and ran her right hand through her short, blond hair.

"Okay?" I shrugged. "Why? What's the matter?"

I tried to recollect if I had had a negative interaction with the patient in 501. *Let's see . . . 501 is an elderly white gentleman who is post-operation day two from a gallbladder removal. He was having a lot of*

pain this morning. Maybe he needs an extra dose of morphine.

"He says he doesn't want a black doctor," she reluctantly voiced. Each member of the lively southwest nursing station ceased their talking and noise production. Silent unease simultaneously afflicted us all. Her pale cheeks began turning red. She continued to avoid eye contact.

I sat up slowly at my computer and clenched my right fist in my left palm. Hot rage began to radiate from my demeanor. "Black doctors aren't good enou—" I started but didn't finish. My *professional judgment* prevented me from expressing the totality of my annoyance. I foolishly believed that sacrificing my youth and dedicating my life to learning to care for the ailing would not only garner societal respect but perhaps even collective acceptance. The piercing and painful truth punctured my naiveté.

I sighed heavily and shook my head, trying to release some of my rising frustration. "That will be fine," I replied sternly. "We'll have him transferred to another provider."

This scenario was actually rather atypical. Most white patients did not mind having a black doctor, or at least they usually did not make their disapproval overtly known. "Are you like a *doctor* doctor?", "We would prefer someone else," or "Where's the *other* doctor?" were some of the inquiries that would abruptly make me consider my race. I obviously do not know the true motivations for these questions, but they made me contemplate my skin hue nonetheless.

A few would mention phrases like "You don't talk like other black people," "You're not like other black people," or "You're not ghetto, though, you know?" I never quite figured out how to respond to these peculiar statements. Typically, I would react by nodding my head and attempting to remain professional. Were these attempts at expressing they were fine with me because I was acceptably *different* than others with my skin tone?

Other patients would make their personal feelings about race or ethnicity known more *peripherally*. For instance, calling the president a "socialist monkey" or an outright "Muslim terrorist" during a routine exam were things I perceived as distasteful and xenophobic.

These racially contemplative encounters remained at the forefront of my mind during my first three years of practicing medicine. Not due to anger, disgust, or the thought that these patients were all racists or bigots. These culturally awkward interactions were infrequent, and I would like to believe they were not always generated due to concerns relating to my darker complexion.

They persisted in my psyche because this was during a time where it seemed society was decidedly more divided. And it often appeared as though the demarcation lines were drawn by race. Heavily debated shootings of unarmed black men by white police officers dominated the news cycles.

Most officers were acquitted. Dramatic black protests and movements were generated to encapsulate new and chronic frustrations with *the system*. Their motivations were often lost in media coverage due to episodes of looting and violence. Other ethnicities tended to dismiss these ideas as antiwhite extremist agendas or simply as an enraged, lawless black mob.

Religiously motivated terrorist bombings and killings throughout the Middle East, Europe, and in the States were seemingly becoming commonplace. Muslim communities came under scrutiny because they were deemed complicit or inactive in preventing these acts. Calls for interrogating Muslim-looking individuals, Islamic neighborhoods, and mosques became louder.

Activist social-media friends, politically divergent family members, and "anti-your-position" coworkers passionately compelled you to be politically, financially, or most often emotionally invested in these and other perpetual, racially complex debates. These societal influences fostered a hypersensitivity to any racially curious interactions I experienced in the workplace.

One day, while I was checking on one of my patients, I overhead two other patients talking. Their rooms were separated by a thin curtain, so their conversation was completely perceptible. In the left bed lay a quiet, surly, elderly black man. He had recently been diagnosed with prostate cancer and refused any form of treatment. He would not speak to the hospital staff (or anyone, really) without continual provocation. As a matter of fact, this was the first time I ever heard him say more than a few words.

In the bed to the right: an

outspoken, blunt, middle-aged white woman. She used to be a nurse, as she frequently reminded all the hospital staff. She was hospitalized because she had an infection in her left foot.

Both of their respective televisions were on CNN. The news channel was covering a story on a hate group's explicit alliance with a nationalist presidential candidate.

"We need a businessman to fix our budget and get America back on track," the woman asserted.

"This fool?" the gruff old man replied, surprising everybody in the room. He began to cough hysterically.

"Yeah, he's got his own money, and it's time for a change in Washington," she insisted. "He's going to create jobs and fix our economy."

"I don't give a fuck about the economy or a damn job if he's going to take me back to the 1960s. I don't have that luxury," he replied.

The woman did not respond.

SUBSISTING WITHOUT SUN

The light rain created a gentle drumming on the windshield. The neighborhood's immaculate streets were bare. I yawned uncontrollably and blinked. My body was reminding me it was beyond my usual bedtime. All the flawless, lavish green yards were well lit by the bright streetlights. Alternating luxury sedans and high-end SUVs were parked in front of each consecutive mini-mansion.

There was something peaceful about tonight.

We pulled up to the massive gold entry gate and waited for the doors to part. I acknowledged the country club's security officer with a casual nod. He reciprocated. I continued on.

I adjusted my pressed white coat as I drove. It was conspicuously displayed on the back of my driver's seat. After years of several would-be police encounters, I realized this maneuver often dissuaded law-enforcement agents from pulling over the "suspicious" black man in the all-black Audi. From time to time, I would still be followed. But they would usually find more interesting pursuits after tailing me for a few minutes.

After a short distance, we turned into the "nice" Kroger down the street from the golf course. I found a vacant parking spot in the left corner and parked.

Isabel caressed my right hand and beamed at me. She was three months pregnant with our first child. And at 11:47 p.m. on a Tuesday night, she desired chicken-noodle soup. So I wearily stumbled out of bed and we pursued the queen's desires all the way to Kroger.

I smiled back at her and kissed her left cheek.

I grabbed the umbrella off the back seat and rushed through the rain toward the store entrance.

The automatic door opened, and a large white man inadvertently struck me with his right shoulder as he hurried from the store.

The jar startled me.

"Oh, sorry." I was half expecting him to take some ownership for the collision.

He glared at me for moment while the potent smell of burnt tobacco engulfed me.

"Fucking nigger," he shouted.

And I woke up.

ABOUT THE AUTHOR

Oba George, MD, is a young African American physician, mentor, and investor who labors with organizations interested in repairing minority economic inequalities. He also has a personal interest in generating healthy multicultural discussions that foster real change in societal racial dynamics.